hurricane
of thoughts

category I

by catrina

iUniverse, Inc.
New York Bloomington

hurricane of thoughts
category 1

iUniverse books may be ordered through booksellers or by contacting:

iUniverse
1663 Liberty Drive
Bloomington, IN 47403
www.iuniverse.com
1-800-Authors (1-800-288-4677)

ISBN: 978-1-4502-3482-5 (sc)
ISBN: 978-1-4502-3481-8 (ebk)

Printed in the United States of America

iUniverse rev. date: 06/18/2010

come walk with me

come walk with me
on the beach we stand; watch the sun kiss the sea

come walk with me
in the park grass; a picnic lunch of fruit and cheese

come walk with me
thru the woods and splash like kids in the creek

come walk with me
to the old oak tree swing; holding hands feeling free

come walk with me
under the stars we will lay; gazing at nature's beauty

come walk with me
in the spring rain; we will dance to a poetic melody

come walk with me
in my arms; i will forever hold you tightly

come walk with me
i will show you a love you thought could never be

lover, my forever

every night we spent together
words you did utter; lover, my forever

shared my heart with only you
you walked away leaving me blue

living in this evil nightmare
how could you have ever cared

unable to hide
tears i've cried

you wanting a second chance
certainly not in my best interest

trying to apologize thru your eyes
just can't forgive your heartless lies

my dreams will not be spent with you
going to share them with someone new

mirror of conspiracy

memory of a window
can clearly see you now
eager to throw stones
rocks from your throne

your crying game
causing so much pain
living a life full of hate
first one out of the gate

drama queen let everyone be
live your own life of misery

accusations, implications, storytelling
lies you are selling

sitting here in this dark room
not contemplating your next move

mirror of conspiracy
you are so blind to see
you mean nothing to me

spiral staircase

so chilled and tangled; hard to breathe
taking advantage of this love i wear on my sleeve

you and i; how were my eyes so blind
disposal of our love; your actions so unkind

my nightmare; you walk away, our life you shun
affair of deceit; the end has only begun

so caught up in your evil hell
i need to snap out of this emotional shell

torn and broken heart has been misplaced
tumbling down a wrought iron spiral staircase

shared hearts

i don't ever want to live without you
like a noon sky without blue

i don't ever want to live without you
like a spring without flowers in bloom

i don't ever want to live without you
like a summer grass without dew

i don't ever want to live without you
like a starry night without the moon

i'm so in love because of you
our shared hearts become one; forever true

poisonous wasteland

living in a poisonous wasteland
waking everyday trying to understand

inside my head; a romantic illusion
thoughts tied up in mass confusion

your hurtful words tearing me apart
tears fall; puddles drown my heart

soul has died; lost without a guide
notorious neglect; from you i want to hide

sounds of madness; so much twisted time
calling to my angels, ready to fly

blood on my hands you cannot erase
for certain; i will not miss this awful place

creeping toward dawn

blue skies are gone; creeping toward dawn

hours in between; dark and full of gloom
nothing left but a cold, lonely room
deep nail scratches to the face
still searching for a better place

blue skies are gone; creeping toward dawn

emotional agony, evil disgrace
wings; flight to heaven's gate
dark sky; white glare of the full moon
raven calls the soul to an empty tomb

blue skies are gone; creeping toward dawn

i cherish you

throughout our lives we walk hand in hand
the two of us together; we know we can

night after night; i hold only you near
deep in my heart i cherish you, my dear

engulfed in your incredible, beautiful, blue eyes
mesmerized by your touch; telling me no lies

all our years of laughter, memories and tears
two souls sharing a true love; it is so very clear

jealousy; our relationship, so many try to test
strength of love; neither of us let them get our best

throughout our lives we walk hand in hand
the two of us together; we know we can

night after night; i hold only you near
deep in my heart i cherish you, my dear

my biggest mistake

daily my eyes shed tears
my thoughts full of demented fears

your inner self so full of hate
my soul and feelings you did rape

dignity; you alone managed to take
our love affair; my biggest mistake

misery that lives on your face
forever love; you have misplaced

darkness of the night falls
another heart damaged by your claws

one candle lit

day after day sitting; tortured pain
staring at the long gravel driveway
our once shared house; now my hiding place
still waiting for your beautiful face

no hope for my emotional rescue
now, my best friend loving you
confused state of mind
myself i struggle; me i cannot find

bottle my only loyal friend
wishing this broken heart would mend
with you my life mattered
heart so torn and tattered

do not need a padded cell
already in my own hell
the old porch swing i sit
night after night; one candle lit

sharing a love

gently holding your hand in mine
waiting for this moment all our life

surrendered our souls to one another
sharing a love, each day gets better

with every spring flower that blooms
it's your affection that brightens my room

not hard to believe this is real
closing my eyes, it's your touch i feel

only your ship i want to sail
true partnership; finally, we prevail

with you, right where i want to be
i will adore you forever; this you will see

each others eyes

unbridled; so free, everyday able to be just you and me
peaceful sharing; right where we both want and need to be

fragrance of beautiful red rose petals fill the room
promise to love one another far past the moon

bottle of bubbling champagne chilling on ice
magical love affair that engulfs our entire lives

reaching to hold hands; anticipation of the next caress
two people that adore the glorious match of togetherness

like stars that twinkle in the darkness of our night
no other relationship has ever felt so very bright

tonight we sit in the glow of flickering candle light
us; so lost in love, staring into each others eyes

my soul went faint

all the days i have traveled alone
wanting to build a loving home
with you; my special someone

wishing one day these dreams
become our long awaited reality

butterflies; the dive they take
as soon as i see your beautiful face
sitting next to one another
goosebumps have taken over

whispering in my ear
loving things you say to me
your affection brings me to my knees
never wanting this amazing feeling to leave

my heart flutters
the reflection in your eyes
a loves desire
every kiss takes me higher

sharing the air we breath
always wanting you with me

lost in the sweet sound of your voice
you have left me no choice
my life is complete
as long as you are with me

cold december morning
our lives we paint
the very day we met
my soul went faint

mirror i stare

your cruel ways; i cannot take anymore
our relationship; ready to part this evil horror

broken bathroom mirror i stare
for myself; i don't even care

emotions; in the devil's lair they lay
my torn soul, leaving your life today

tears weep; splattered across the cold tile floor
stop a beating heart; no more life of scorn

blood drips, flowing down the drain
dull razor blade taking away the pain

delicate burn

movies
bookstores
libraries
dinners

times we spend together

just friends we say
maybe one day that will change

on the same page
so many things
thoughts of you
all over my memory

watching you sleep

do you have a clue
how much i love you

hugs goodbye
look deeper into my eyes
a silence that
will never be broken

our lips kiss
a fantasy
tucked away
in a midnight dream

delicate burn
my heart on fire
you are my desire

morphing

are we just morphing thru time

heartless people living off of someone else's dime
the vatican committing sexual crimes
wasted lives; innocent people doing time
organized religion living hypocritical lives
our own government poisoning us from the inside
why does everyone seem to be so, so blind

are we really just morphing thru our time

flight of an angel

you care for me
you help me see
you are a part of my presence
always keeping residence

over the trees you fly
so very high
riding on the wind
committing no sin

dancing on the clouds
wings spread out
lifting yourself; touching a rainbow
knowing you are my guardian angel

engravings of wrath

last candle lit; nothing left but a puddle of wax and a piece of wick
for far too many years falling for your hateful tricks

words spew across your lips tearing me apart
like a knife; you cut deep at my bleeding heart

colorful sunrise; a less sparkle of dew covers the grass
sole witness to your evil engravings of wrath

trying to remember the happy days, when you were mine
beautiful flowers in a row; each petal dies, one at a time

a cemetery of counterfeit feelings; you tumble and fall
left to pick up the pieces; this time building my own wall

friends and lovers

all the tears i have cried
you have managed to wipe dry

heartbreak, years on the mend
your love i feel is heaven sent

as our time has come to pass
everyday, nothing but a blast

wonderful relationship discovered
greatest love of all; friends and lovers

do that

calling me your world
same thing i've already heard

less than intelligent conversation; not what i seek
do that; and our relationship will be weak

living with yourself in a distraught past
do that; our relationship will not last

no compassion; it's not living in your heart
do that; this relationship is over before it starts

calling me your world
same thing i've already heard

tone deaf and off key

broken violin strings
your song you tried to sing

missing ivory piano keys
your lies; thought i could not see

worn record player stuck on repeat
gave you my heart; for keeps

with your shadow you dance
you used your last chance

wonderful daydream

drifting far away into a daydream

you and i playing like children, carefree

skipping thru the conservatory, smelling every rose we see

on the beach, holding hands, wading our feet

listening to a one man band playing music in the park

running thru the museum viewing colorful works of art

holding the chains tight as we swing as high as the sky

sad ending to a romantic movie, we both cry

the observatory, we gaze at the stars on a moonlit night

for hours on end we just sit and talk by candle light

here we can do absolutely anything

because it is my wonderful daydream

ketchup mustard

you cannot live a life
if you have not lived in misery

do not need potions
and a boiling pot
no voodoo doll
pins and needles

no drugs to help me heal
life's last sequel
management by stress
actions we need to second guess

our thought process

chapels fall

a butterfly
a ladybug
a penny, heads up

chapels fall

a four leaf clover
when will the hate be over

a penny, heads up
a ladybug
a butterfly

chapels fall

sweetest of dreams

enjoying every moment of this wonderful feeling
every bit of my heart; your ways are stealing

each day of your life i will be there
the happiest of hearts, because i care

long awaited affair, our miracle of love
sent down from the beautiful heavens above

daydreaming about your softest touch
you have captured my soul; i love you so much

the sweetest of dreams has come true
spending the rest of my life with you

how lucky can one woman be
you by my side, always with me

my message to you; believe it to be true
each day that passes i keep falling more in love with you

helpless hostage

every night a horrible fight
myself, i have managed to lose sight
it is so hard to breathe
my feelings you did deceive

a noose around my neck
so sick of your idle threats
all of my energy exhausted
no longer your helpless hostage

emotional ending, broken heart
your many promised fresh starts
countless overrated words of forever love
all my eyes can see is a grave of doves

to the bottom i've sunk, a low life
me inside; time to put up a fight
emptiness consumes my soul
leave me alone; please, just let me go

sweet better half

your drum
beats in my heart

your guitar
strums my soul

your fire
feeds my desire

beautiful angel
you fly me higher

you make me smile
you make me laugh
you are my sweet, sweet better half

breaths are suffocating

shadow moves about our room
wishing it belonged to you
shallow screams; restless sleep
missing you lying next to me

walls closing in; my breaths are suffocating
night after night; putting up a fight
tossing and turning
your love i am yearning

chest sinks deep
heart caught in the coiled springs
dreams turn into nightmares
head buried in a pillow of tears

fighting the satin sheets
another night trying to fall asleep
crying
until my eyes close without dying

happiness reigns

past life of growing pains and stepping stones; not a waste

happiness reigns; written all over the smile on my face

into this loving relationship i dive; not a moment of haste

truest love i feel for you; this can never be replaced

your soul trembling touch; takes me to a higher place

our kisses; even when we are apart, i can still taste

no longer a fairytale of unobtainable dreams i need to chase

your marvelous way and display of love; my heart you did take

start of a new romance; this life spent with you, my soul mate

moving on

you lust
you love
you hurt
you cry
you smile
you frown
you feel like your life has been turned upside down
you learn from your mistakes
you take risks
you take chances
you build walls
you tear them down to build them all over again

you; are a part of me
you; i will never forget

winding road

traveling along a long, dark, winding road
lost; i cannot find my own way back home

missing you; so empty, feelings are stone
stuck on repeat; listening to our song
memories of you dance within my soul
morbid thoughts of your concrete tombstone
shivers consume my body; overtaken by cold
in my dreams, it is you i forever hold
my friend; i promised you would never be alone

traveling along a long, dark, winding road
lost; i cannot find my own way back home

love to hate

slow death
evil
rat race
running in place

do not love to hate

dark sunshine
souls missing
everyone doing nothing
complaining about something

do not love to hate

living dead
ego's fed
silent screams
dancing in my head

do not love to hate

shallow graves dug deep
under a heap of concrete
restless sleep
keeping me in grief

do not love to hate

tough love
bright light
eclipse of the mind
humanity, we need to find

do not love to hate

matter of trust

convinced; a lifetime partner was merely a fantasy
but being with you takes me away to a world of ecstasy

every single moment we spend together
our lives just keep getting better and better

truth and honesty, this is the way it is meant to be
true love; no hidden agendas, no tricks up the sleeve

never, nothing, no one will ever come between us
loving one another; it is simply a matter of trust

our hearts living in a field of future dreams
conquering a wonderful shared love; just you and me

at night holding you tight; falling asleep in my arms
anticipation of morning; waking to your beautiful face and charm

when we are apart; only you consume my thoughts
your kiss and touch; never imagined loving you so much

within my heart everything that encompasses love
falling hard for you; the love of my life you have become

so certain that there aren't anymore walls to climb
you and your amazing soul already live inside of mine

mystic journey

beautiful things we hear and see
natures amazing show for you and me
birds harmonizing every sunrise
fireflies dancing in the night sky

you are my sunshine on a cloudy day
a crisp clean spring shower in may
white rose petals that flower
fragrant bloom on a morning of summer

amazing color your soul radiates
like a valley of trees and the changing leaves
craving the love that flows from your heart
cold december morning feeling your warmth

beautiful smile that adorns your precious face
soft lips anticipation of the next kiss
stunning blue eyes as deep as the shallows of the sea
mystic journey of love we travel; just you and me

paralyzed

paint waring thin
can i trust a relationship again
the weathered worn shutters
talking to you i stutter

every step i take
telling myself no wait
resembling the beauty of a dove
clawing myself toward love

getting older afraid of the next step
you i do not want to second guess
not believing this to be true
meeting someone as incredible as you

wanting to right the wrong
listening to your amazing song
marvelous piece of art
you have paralyzed my heart

finally, at last

every little thing the two of us do
all my thoughts are consumed by you

i so adore the wonderful person you are
amazing what you have done, erasing my scars

most cozy in your surroundings
these feelings, my heart is pounding

wrapped up in your contagious smile
my lover, something i haven't felt in awhile

jumping from cloud to cloud
i love you, shouting it out loud

amazing eyes sparkle when you look at me
all i see is you in my future dreams

found what has been missing from my past
beautiful you in my life; finally, at last

even without you

even without you

the sun will shine
the birds will sing
the rain will pour
the thunder will roar
the seasons will pass
the grass will grow
the waters will flow
the wind will blow
the moon will glow
the stars will twinkle
the flowers will bloom

even without you

the person you are

started out as a friendship
resulting in a dream
holding you in my arms
i can clearly see you with me

the love i have for you
is beyond reality
you are deep within my heart
this feeling will never part

your positive manner
your non-judgemental ways
taking on the world so brave
much of you i crave

thinking of you everyday
why must you be so far away
seems like millions of miles
missing your daily smiles

sitting alone in this candle lit room
admiring you from afar
wanting you to know
i love the person you are

my noose

lost in your eyes not hearing the lies
living without you i want to die
silent screams taking over my brain
thoughts racing down a track like a speeding train

rung, by rung, by rung i climb
pulling myself closer to the sky
trying to let go of my tortured pain
tugging desperately at sane

just trying to reach the door
dragging myself across the floor
river of tears soak the carpet
you left me so heartbroken

every single room i crawl thru
still carries the scent of you
sitting by the old oak tree feeling blue
clutching tightly; memories of you, my noose

sounds of spring

crystallized snowflakes melting, loosing shape
water dancing down icicles; puddles filling space

dark cloudy days gone by
admiring the bright yellow sun in the sky

rays shining down on my face
so lucky for this marvelous place

birds chirping in the trees, singing a romantic melody
mother nature's magnificent display of change

wishing you were here with me
enjoying the beautiful sounds of spring

blue steel

alive; thinking you are sane
death reigns in the form of pain

pieces missing from life's show
no one knows how far i will go

searching for a path of escape
to the skies i gaze, praying to saints

blue steel; chamber, an evil wheel

flesh and bone, help me please
rush of death, cut to the knees

blue steel; chamber, an evil wheel

alive; thinking you are sane
death reigns in the form of pain

hell i roam

bitter; enough, heart so stuck
lost in a disturbed, emotional rut

sad story of an over abundance of pain
innocent life; trying to explain

falling into dawn's early light
losing the battle; no more fight

social disease; who do i please
your tainted love; heart of tease

crow flies; another tear drop
poisonous parasite; just stop

stripped down; flesh and bone
lonely; in this hell i roam

fool in love; a slaughtered dove
chasing my soul back to where it was

one step at a time

raindrops drip from the blooms of the trees
like the tears that stream down my cheeks

crescent moon shines in the dark sky
slowly mending this broken heart of mine

alone, sailing the roughest of the deep blue seas
everyday learning something new about me

one step at a time; dancing across the sand
taking a deep breath; forgetting our romance

promises in the dark

promises in the dark
you alone captured my heart
your words turned to lies
tears filled my eyes

you paved my way to happiness
in an instant made my life a mess
unexpected rain of tears
you leaving after many years

smell of death in the air
no way you ever cared
my beautiful mistake
this heart you did take

off to never, never land
here alone i will stand
some things are not meant for keeps
night after night i visit you in my dreams

my lucky charm

holding you in my arms
my lucky charm

into your eyes i stare
fingers running thru your hair

soft lips
your breath taking kiss

like a raging river
you make my body quiver

i have fallen deep
within my soul, you, i will keep

holding on tight
ready for this lifetime ride

dreams do come true
here i lay next to you

tragedy

parts of me hit the wall
surviving an emotional fall

your late night calls need to cease
better off without you; i have found my peace

seeing the difference between night and day
not falling for the evil ways you try to play

for me; i am no longer last in line
finally; finally, able to leave you behind

from the bottom of your heart; you love me
you; let me go long before this so called tragedy

parts of you hit the wall
you will survive your emotional fall

corner i cower

with you; so in love i fell
chained to your evil spell

our abandoned dark bedroom
your shadow dances with the full moon

trying to escape your emotional power
in this frigid corner I cower

surrender

years complicated by pain
crossing the finish line of sane
heartbeat skips
lovely feeling of bliss

no longer afraid
mastered the game
your hand in mine
ready for the love of a lifetime

your eyes pull me near
no doubts, no fear
taking my breath away
always wanting you to stay

you will shine
in this heart of mine
to you my dear
white flag i surrender

another lullaby

hatred in the sun
are we undone

cold, then we die
where is the reason

why

our pain, understanding
distant tears

why

society cries
another lullaby

why

hatred in the sun
cold, when we die

where is the reason

my forever lies

gorgeous smile that paints your face
takes me away to that magical place

no longer a deep mystery
feeling the love you have for me

listening to your beautiful song
for this; i have waited so long

in your sparkling blue eyes
with you; my forever lies

own bloody pain

living a life of sadness and gloom
all alone in this frigid dark room
across the hardwood floor i crawl
clawing my way up the wall
thru the rainy, fogged window i stare
does anyone in my life even care

looking for love in all the wrong places
everyone the same, staring at too many faces
lying in my own bloody pain
friends desperately helping me toward sane
everyday of my life is where i want you to be
love of my life i so wish you could see

memory

your voice, your told lies
had me trapped in your eyes
beautiful bright red smile
nothing more than pure evil

climbing back on the train
thoughts pollute my brain
trying to stay on track
stealing my heart back

only one chance with me
you thought you had many
in you; all that i can see
simply nothing more than a memory

because of you

because of you
realizing love can be true
feeling of loneliness
no longer exists

in my mind
with you, someone so kind
thoughts of you dance
finding romance

every time i look into your eyes
unexpected feeling of butterflies
heart no longer blue
lost in this heaven with you

i thought I heard you call

the sunrise; your beautiful eyes

the tide rolls in and out

the love we share is unselfish
without a doubt

holding hands

the sand beneath our toes
when we kiss our hearts glow

the sunset
another beautiful day well spent

falling asleep in one another's arms
the sunrise
the pouring rain
i wake again

wiping tears from my eyes
and then i realize

it is merely another dream

the waves crash against the sea wall
i thought i heard you call

---

bid you goodbye

left your debris
floating on my dead sea
why can't you hear my plea
please just let me be

sun rises, sun sets
my life a complete mess
one heartbeat at a time
lost in my paralyzed mind

no spark left in my flame
future remains uncertain
one thing for myself i will do, not a lie
from my broken heart i bid you goodbye

foiled master plan

voices in the head
already dead
trying to understand
foiled master plan

razor blade, knife or gun

death creeps into dreams
only solution it seems
life of hate
determining my fate

cure or disease

voices in the head
already dead
try to understand
foiled master plan

razor blade, knife, or gun

friendship

20 years pass
blast from the past
unexpected chance
felt like a friendship lost

turning back time
stolen moments of belly laughs
with wild abandonment
a matter of trust

we were always on the same bus

room to breathe

bones chilled; suffering from a broken soul
fooling me; questioning how i didn't know

infamous lying, back tracking pattern
leaving my heart in this hell; scattered

your silent signals i could not read
cheating ways; looking for room to breathe

this life; living without your kiss
nasty taste of bittersweet bliss

our love; a mirage in your heart
waking; looking for a fresh start

if only you knew

how hard i really fell for you
your selfishness; if only you knew

games you play; you fan the flames
temper; unkind words always laying blame

heart pulled apart from the inside
love affair has become an emotional parasite

silent screams penetrate these walls
your constant i'm sorry; my hurt calls

living your life off of people you know
no support from you; time for me to go

this love is poison; a harsh reality
sick of your me, me, me mentality

listening to your last song sung
this one sided relationship; i am so done

role you play is nothing but take away
leaving your heartless soul; leaving you today

my life i control; my new beginning
black and white; i am writing our ending

a cloud

needing wings
so i can be free

where to roam
this is not my home

living on the streets
trying to make ends meet

sun rises, sun sets
trapped under this pavement

cold, lost and sad
eternal sleep; a cloud

picnic lunch

old truck starts
picnic lunch packed
fishing poles stacked
driving thru the countryside

colorful leaves cover the trees
sun shines thru the windows
the wind blows our hair
spending the day together

away from the sadness
far from the madness

creating our own beautiful day
come what may
not a dream
just you and me

barefoot wading in the creek bed
hand and hand
laughing and splashing
acting like kids

sitting in the grass
leaning against a shade tree
taking in the surrounding beauty
mother nature's marvelous painting

castle of doom

white picket fence
on the cold ground like matchsticks

overgrown grass covered fields
heart wasn't born with a shield

curtains now closed
last day of your show

castle of doom
once where flowers bloomed

falling into you

lost in your love and affection
our hearts headed in the right direction

beautiful thoughts of you consume my mind
goosebumps and a stomach full of butterflies

when our lips kiss; my soul melts
most incredible feeling i have ever felt

your gorgeous love keeps me warm
my beating heart protected from harm

falling into you; my heart, so deep
you always a part of me; for keeps

cannot imagine my life without you
a lifetime romance forever true

together again

the amazing love you and i display
our open hearts; we, are on our way

a sincere voice telling me no lies
your beautiful soul dancing in my eyes

your kiss, i feel on my lips
wanting to caress your body, you i miss

at night; i think, when we are apart
it is only you that holds my heart

for miles and miles i would walk
to hold your hand and hear you talk

within my dreams you will live
until; you and i are together again

pouring rain

walking away; taking my pride with your lies
beautiful love affair; disguised in angel eyes

hard to walk thru this pouring rain
wading thru the damage of past pain

passing years; pails of wasted tears
praying for my gray skies to clear

me; destroying myself on the inside
tired of hearing useless tears penetrate my eyes

keeper of my dreams

keeper of my dreams
you are all i will ever need
i love your way
every night and day

thru all of the seasons
my love will grow for many reasons
no longer locked in my chains
ready for this life of change

closing my eyes
i can see your smile for miles
lost in the moments
you leave me breathless

a gift sent from above
you will always be my true love
you are all i will ever need
keeper of my dreams

circus is in town

the ups and downs
the twists and turns
let the games begin

the webs you weave
the way you deceive
take another spin

you are not a mastermind

dear game player
find another way
you are a manipulator
it is as plain as night and day

forgiving the unforgivable

cold is the night air
mist in my blank stare
losing my direction
falling for your affection

hostage of an old love affair
what you did; why do i still care
your cheating, your lies
living a life in disguise

feeling sorry for my weary mind
knowing it is me i need to find
giving you too much of my time
taking control of this life of mine

going to trust my heart
tomorrow my fresh start
finally letting you go
forgiving the unforgivable

different shades of green

the rolling brown fields of the farm
overdue anticipation of spring's charm

clear blue sky; not a cloud in sight
delightful afternoon; sun shining ever so bright

woods full of bare naked trees
slowly dressing; different shades of green

lightning strikes and the thunder rolls
rain falling from the sky forming puddles

each drop feeds all sorts of plants across the plains
alas; winter is over, welcome to the days of spring

alone travels

like a boat without a sail
another relationship failed

reaching for the life preserver floating on the water
how could you do this; my heart and mind wonder

for once our true love; i did bow
trying to survive this emotional ride; learning how

taking control of my feelings; being stern
in the past it was your love i did yearn

slowly dropping the anchor
learning to let go of the anger

mast high in the sky; i sail the waters of the deep blue sea
drowning these sad feelings; letting my soul free

so very close

day you left; i needed you most
hearts forever; so very close

in your plan; i was your silly pawn
my very last breath; i will be gone

like a crater on the moon
my broken heart; your tomb

our last love note; do not contact me
without you; i can finally see

found strength, found able
left my wedding ring on our table

if i was

if i was rain
i would sing a melody
dance on your window pane
wash all your sorrows away

if i was a fire
i would burn forever
always keeping you warm
in this cruel world of cold

if i was a key
i would unlock your heart
show you a true love
one that will never part

if i had wings
soar thru the sky
i would fly
and visit all your dreams

if i was the sun
i would shine upon your marvelous soul
hang out in the blue sky
and just stare at your beautiful smile

if i was a book
i would read a wonderful story
of you and i falling in love
like two morning doves

you are my sun
you are my moon
my love
i would do anything for you

obituary

dock we sit wading our feet
every single kiss; our hearts skip a beat

sun glares into your beautiful eyes
your smile glistens for miles

shallow swims; ladder is broken
steps toward my own mistake

on this dock
i will sit and wait

air i breathe

deep within your amazing blue eyes my feelings fly
you a daily reminder; no more lonely nights nor tears to cry

with you; our entire lives i want us to share
everyday showing one another how much we care

floating together in a magnificent sea of love
gliding thru the clouds like two morning doves

colorful sunrise; whispers of i love you; now we both know
beautiful flowers in bloom and the spring breeze blows

two souls meet with the help of an angel's prayer
hearts beat to a beautiful song; our love always there

you and your wonderful heart is all i want and need
for i would give you the very air i breathe

diary of pain

mean words and your evil bruising
my restless, haunting memory

lost love; a powerful, emotional weapon
sin you committed still frozen to my skin

sacrificing my beating heart
crushed, broken and torn apart

it is 3:03; spending another night of lonely
praying to the sky above; your love so phony

my confused thoughts will not let me sleep
wasted time spent just laying here as i weep

this shattered life; driving me insane
tear smeared ink; a diary of pain